A Special Gift

for:
_____

from:
_____

date:
_____

Stories, Sayings, and Scriptures to Encourage and Inspire

hugs™
for
teens

COTT
RIPPAYNE

rsonalized
riptures by
eAnn Weiss

HOWARD
PUBLISHING CO.

Our purpose at Howard Publishing is to:

- *Increase faith* in the hearts of growing Christians
- *Inspire holiness* in the lives of believers
- *Instill hope* in the hearts of struggling people everywhere

Because He's coming again!

Hugs for Teens © 2001 by Scott Krippayne
All rights reserved. Printed in the United States of America

Published by Howard Publishing Co., Inc.,
3117 North 7th Street, West Monroe, LA 71291-2227

04   05   06   07   08   09   10   10

Paraphrased Scriptures © 2000 LeAnn Weiss,
3006 Brandywine Dr., Orlando, FL 32806; 407-898-4410

Edited by Philis Boultinghouse
Interior design by Stephanie Denney

Library of Congress Cataloging-in-Publication Data
Krippayne, Scott, 1970–
    Hugs for teens : stories, sayings, and scriptures to encourage and inspire / Scott
Krippayne ; personalized scriptures by LeAnn Weiss.
       p. cm.
    ISBN 1-58229-213-2
    1. Teenagers—Religious life. I. Weiss, LeAnn. II. Title.

BV4531.3 .K75 2001
242'.63—dc21   2001047031

Scripture quotations not otherwise marked are taken from the Holy Bible, New International Version. Copyright © 1973, 1978, 1984 International Bible Society. Used by permission of Zondervan Bible Publishers. Other Scriptures quoted from The Holy Bible, New King James Version (NKJV), © 1982 by Thomas Nelson, Inc.

Contents

For information about
Scott Krippayne's newest CD, see page 122.

Reaching Out

O N E

1

Hey, even when things
aren't meeting up to your
expectations and plans,
**never doubt that I will fulfill My
unique purpose for you.**
I'll never abandon you. When you love Me and
are called according to My higher purpose,
you can trust Me to make all things,
even the disappointments and struggles,
work out for your benefit!

Working behind the scenes for you,
Your All-Powerful God

—from Psalm 138:8; Romans 8:28

What are you afraid of? What do you worry about? Are you concerned about the test you have next week? Or are you afraid that people won't like you, that you won't be accepted? What keeps you up at night—lying in bed, staring at the ceiling?

When you start to worry, remember that God loves you as you are. He's not impressed by how you dress or the people you hang out with. He's not going to love you any less if you don't ace that next test. "Who of you by worrying can add a single hour to his life?" (Matthew 6:27).

Jesus reminds us that worrying doesn't really get us anywhere. And He has told us that if we will just come to Him, He will give us relief from our burdens (see Matthew 11:28). We can ask for His strength to live life one day, one step at a time, and He will gladly give it to us. "Do not worry about tomorrow, for tomorrow will worry about itself" (Matthew 6:34). Keep your eyes focused on God and the love He has for you, and say to yourself, "I can do all things through Christ who strengthens me" (Philippians 4:13 NKJV).

Attitude is the mind's paintbrush. It can color a situation gloomy and gray, or cheerful.... In fact, attitudes are more important than facts.

—Mary C. Crowley

First Day

Theresa had always looked forward to the first day of school, but this year was different. Due to her father's recent job change, she and her family had moved across the country to a new town and a new neighborhood. They had barely had a chance to meet the people next-door. It was hard enough to leave the friends she'd known for thirteen years, but right before school started? Did her parents really expect her to adjust?

She didn't even want to get out of bed. Getting up meant going to school, and that meant groups and cliques that were already well established—and that she wasn't a part of. She didn't know a soul. She had no friends. Who would she talk to? Who would she hang out with? The thought of walking through the halls and not seeing any familiar faces terrified her. Maybe she could be sick. No, her parents would see right through that one, and she'd still have to face her first day at a new school sometime. It might as well be today.

While trying to decide what to wear, Theresa caught a glimpse of herself in the mirror. Of course, today would have to be a bad hair day. *This day is not starting out well,* she thought to herself. But on with the inevitable. After a quick breakfast, she grabbed her things and headed down the street to the corner where the bus would pick her up.

In the distance, she could see three girls laughing about something. As Theresa got closer, the girls shot a brief look her way and then continued on with their conversation. Finally the bus arrived. Theresa stepped on and sat alone. The ride was bumpy, and it seemed like an eternity until the bus pulled up in front of the school.

First Day

Theresa climbed off the bus with no idea where to go. She tried to blend in as best she could and followed the other kids inside. Her old school was much smaller. This one was a sea of lockers. How would she ever figure out where hers was? After quite a lengthy search, she found it— number 454. She dropped off some of her things and began the trek down the long hallway to first period, trying desperately not to bump into anyone.

She had made it through the first three or so hours. The classes weren't so bad. She could simply find a desk and sit there. The teachers pretty much just went over class rules and grading policies—no serious learning was expected the first day. But now it was lunchtime, and the question of where to eat was looming large. The groups would form quickly, as friends were eager to catch up with one another after a long summer. Theresa was keenly aware of the fact that she had no one to catch up with—no one to sit with at all. She wondered if she had ever reached out to any of the new students where she used to go to school. Now she was the new kid, and it was harder than she had ever imagined.

She found a place alone in the corner and sat down with her lunch. Just as she started to eat, she saw three girls approaching. They were the girls from the bus stop.

"Do you mind if we join you?" said the one in front.

Mind? Please was more like it. "Not at all," Theresa replied.

"This is usually where we sit for lunch, and we just thought that since we saw you at the bus stop this morning and since you are sitting here now, it must be fate or something," said another. "Maybe we're supposed to be friends."

"How's your first day?" said the third, a redhead.

"OK, I guess," Theresa replied. "We just moved here three days ago."

"Where are you from?"

"Tennessee, born and raised."

"My family moved here from Missouri last year. I remember how hard it was—starting school and not knowing anybody. I just wanted to crawl into a hole at lunchtime. But over time I met a few really nice people, including these two."

"We haven't even introduced ourselves yet," the first one said. "My name is Rachael, and this is Mariya and Megan."

"Hi, I'm Theresa."

And with that, new friendships were formed, and Theresa's day was looking up. They chatted about their classes and giggled about which boys they thought were cute. They reminisced about their summers, each sharing their stories of suntans and various adventures, basically talking their way through lunch.

"Maybe we can pick this up after school," Mariya suggested. "I've got to get to class right now. Let's meet outside the cafeteria at the end of the day—that means you too, Theresa."

They parted as each went to her next class. Theresa kept going over the random encounter in her head as she sat through fourth period. Did that really just happen? She actually had fun at lunch! Who would've thought that her first day would actually turn out to be enjoyable? It almost seemed too good to be true. Megan, Mariya, and Rachael were really nice—and thoughtful.

At the end of the day, Theresa stopped by her locker to pick up her belongings and was the first of the girls to arrive outside the cafeteria. She wondered if the others would remember. But right then, Megan came up behind her and gave her a hug.

"Congratulations, you made it through the first day!" Megan said.

"Thanks, congrats to you too," Theresa said with a smile.

Rachael and Mariya weren't far behind, and the four friends headed out to the bus.

For Theresa, the ride home was quite a bit different from the bus trip that morning. She now had people to sit with and new friends to talk to. The time went by much more quickly than the ride to school. The girls talked and laughed the entire way back to their neighborhood. They exited the bus and began the walk to their respective houses. One by one, they said their good-byes and exchanged quick hugs followed by a "See you tomorrow."

Living the farthest from the bus stop, Theresa was the last one home. She walked in the door with a smile. Her mother asked how her first day went. "It was OK," came the reply. But Theresa knew it was far better than just OK. Over dinner she told her parents the story—how she'd started off dreading this day but ended up meeting some new friends and genuinely having a great day.

As she crawled into bed that night, Theresa thanked God for bringing the new friends into her life and asked God to help her be the kind of friend who reaches out to others. She was truly grateful for the effort the three girls had made. They didn't have to do it; they could've simply gone on with their day. But they chose to reach out to a stranger, and they made a huge difference in Theresa's day. She closed her eyes and smiled again. She couldn't wait for tomorrow.

Sharing Love

TWO

You are forever loved!
Be convinced that nothing you
could ever do, say, or think could
ever stop Me from loving you—
Absolutely nothing and no one in the
entire world can separate you from My
unconditional and indescribable love!
My empowering love helps you overcome all
circumstances, colossal blunders, and mistakes.
Just ask Me, and I'll remove your mess-ups
as far as the east is from the west.

Loving you always,
Your God of Forgiveness

—from Romans 8:35–39; Psalm 103:12

Have you ever had a bad day? OK, not just a bad day, but one of those days when you're sure that staying in bed would've been a much better option. The kind of day when everything goes wrong—from the moment you wake up until you climb back under your covers at night. It seems like those days can't end soon enough. All you want to do is crawl into a hole, hide from the world, and wait for tomorrow to arrive. Have you ever had one of those days?

On a day like that, the words "I love you" or "I understand" are priceless. They help soothe the ache and remind us that we're not alone. And when a friend reaches out to give you a hug, it may be just the touch you need to make it to the next moment. We have a God who whispers those precious words to us every day—"I love you; I understand"—a God who reaches out to embrace us and hold us close through the toughest of times.

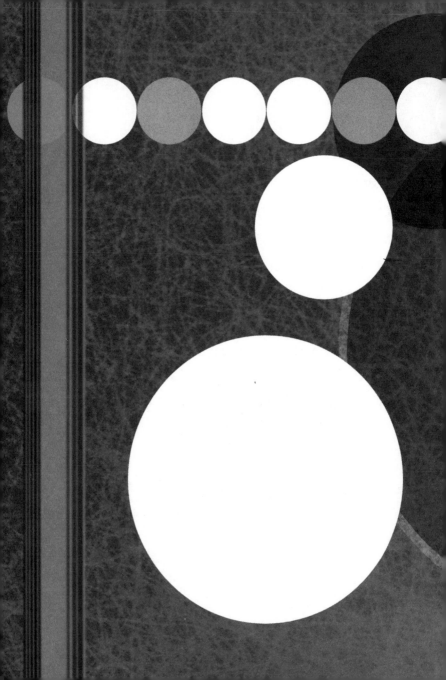

No matter what sin we
have committed, no matter
how terrible it may be,
God loves us.

—Billy Graham

Car Wreck

After sixteen years of waiting, Brian finally got his driver's license. He had practiced and studied, and he knew his stuff. But, still, he barely passed with a seventy—the lowest possible passing score. Aside from a nerve-induced test score, he was a good driver. What he lacked in experience, he made up for in responsibility. His parents trusted him.

Brian didn't have a car of his own, but he was able to borrow the family car for various outings. His parents believed in starting slow, so there were some rather strict rules regarding auto usage—things like having only one passenger in the car and not driving after dark or in bad weather. But as the weeks went by and the trust level increased, Brian was given more automotive freedom.

Just about two months after receiving his license, Brian asked if he could take the family car and spend a day at the state fair with a friend. His parents happily gave their consent. So with that, Brian pulled out of the driveway and waved good-bye to his parents.

"Thanks so much," he yelled out the window as he set off for his friend Colin's house.

Colin didn't live far—maybe ten or fifteen minutes away. And it wasn't long before both boys were buckled in and on their way downtown to the fair. It was a gorgeous day, so they naturally had the windows down and the stereo up.

Their drive was on a winding two-lane road with a few small hills but certainly not what anyone would consider a dangerous route. They followed the road to the left, slowly curved back to the right, and then proceeded up toward the crest of a hill. There was an intersection at the top, but the boys had the right of way. Brian thought he noticed a Chevy Nova on the left waiting at a stop sign, but he didn't give it much thought. As the boys reached the intersection, the Nova pulled forward. All of a sudden there was a collision, and the boys were spun around, coming to rest in the opposite lane. It all happened so fast.

"Are you OK?" Brian asked his buddy.

"I think so. What just happened?" Colin responded.

"We just got broadsided."

Brian tried to roll up the window, but the glass had completely shattered inside the door. Slowly the boys began to regain their senses. The Nova was in the middle of the intersection, and the front end was considerably damaged. But everyone appeared to be all right—a little shaken but no major injuries.

Brian unbuckled his seat belt and tried to open the door. Finally, with a healthy shove, it gave way. He gingerly stepped outside to assess the damage. It looked as if the entire left side of the car were one big dent. The windows on the driver's side were in a thousand pieces, and the doors were crunched.

"So much for the car," he mumbled under his breath.

But all things considered, he was grateful—things could've been much worse. A quick prayer of thanks seemed inadequate, but it was all he could muster at the moment.

Brian's mind began to fill with questions and confusion. *How could this have happened? I hope it wasn't my fault. It couldn't be…or could it? Could I have missed a stop sign? No, we didn't have a stop sign. Was I going too fast? I should have seen it coming. Could I have been a more defensive driver?*

He continued to wrestle with his thoughts. *Where did that car come from anyway? The crash seemed to have such force. Did the Nova stop at the sign and then start, or did it simply run right through?*

And then it came. *My parents! How will I explain this to my parents? They will never believe it wasn't my fault. I'm such a young driver. There must have been something I could've done to avoid the accident. But that's what it was, wasn't it—an accident? What will they think? What are they going to say?*

By this time, the police had arrived and were surveying the scene. They took statements from Brian and Colin regarding what happened, and they questioned the other driver as well. A tow truck showed up for the Nova: That car wasn't going anywhere on its own. Brian's car, his parents' Camry, was still drivable—barely. Before long, the tow company had the Chevy hooked up, and they drove off. The police had all they needed for the report but waited to leave until Brian and Colin were on their way.

The boys slowly climbed into the damaged vehicle and headed back to Colin's place. The fair was unthinkable under the circumstances. Brian thought it best to get Colin home safe before making the journey to his own house.

When they reached Colin's residence, Colin climbed out of the car and wished his shaken friend luck.

"Be honest and don't worry; it wasn't your fault," Colin said, trying to be upbeat.

"I know…I think. But it's not going to be easy to break this to them. It's *their* car."

"Hang in there, and call me when you're off restriction," Colin said with a smile as he waved good-bye.

Brian pointed the car in the direction of his house and drove. When he got closer to home, he tried to think of ways to deliver the bad news. He thought about starting with, "It wasn't my fault, and I'm OK." That would cover the essentials. Someone else's insurance would cover the cost of the repairs, and there were no injuries. It seemed simple enough. But in his mind, Brian could see the look on his father's face when he broke the news. He concluded that in no way was this going to be a pleasant experience.

As he pulled into his neighborhood, Brian realized he needed to speak to his parents, as difficult as that would be, *before* they had a chance to see the car. But as he neared the house, he saw his parents outside working in the front yard. This was the worst possible scenario. From the direction he was coming, he would drive right past them, the demolished side of the vehicle in plain sight, even before he pulled into the driveway. It was awful. They would see everything before he had a chance to speak, let alone explain.

He saw their jaws drop as he rolled in front of the house. There was no escape. *How bad was this going to be? How would they react?* Their open mouths were the first indication. He dreaded the encounter. Brian shut the car off, and before he could climb out, his mother was at the window.

"Are you hurt?" she asked frantically.

Brian could hear the worry in his mother's voice, and he assured her that he was OK.

"You all right?" asked his father. "It looks pretty serious. You sure you're OK?"

"Yeah, Dad, I'm fine. I'm really sorry about the car."

"Don't worry about the car; we can get it fixed. We're just thankful you're all right."

Did he hear his father right? The car didn't seem to matter; *he* mattered. Unbelievable.

Brian described what had happened, trying to recount every detail.

"It wasn't your fault, Son—just an accident—nothing you could've done. We're just thankful that you're not hurt."

Brian couldn't remember ever hearing such compassion in his father's voice.

"Accidents are going to happen sometimes," his father added. "We're just glad everyone is OK."

Brian could hardly believe his ears. He knew his parents loved him, and he knew they cared. But in the midst of this circumstance, their love was so evident. Their responses overflowed with it. They loved him! And he could so plainly see it—almost touch it! They embraced. Brian's mother and father held him tightly, as only parents can do. Brian was grateful. He saw the evidence of a love he could not explain. He loved his parents and wanted to please them. They loved him no matter what. This kind of love didn't depend on what he did or didn't do. They simply loved. It was the closest thing to unconditional love he had ever seen. And it was directed toward him. Amazing.

"You still want to go to the fair?" inquired his mom.

"You're not serious," replied Brian.

"Why not? You've been through quite a bit today; you probably need to have some fun."

"OK," Brian finally relented, "but only if you drive."

Facing Fears

THREE

You can do it!
Live wisely, making the most
of every opportunity, as you run
with endurance the race
I've marked out especially for you.
You can do everything I've called you to do
because Christ strengthens you.
I'll faithfully complete the good work
I've started in you.

Encouraging you,
Your Heavenly Father

—from Ephesians 5:15–16; Hebrews 12:1
Philippians 4:13; 1:6

If you watched the 2000 Summer Olympics, you may have seen the incredible moment when a young swimmer from Africa was competing in a preliminary heat of the one hundred-meter freestyle. Due to the false starts of his competitors, he was swimming alone in the water. He wasn't terribly fast, and it was evident he wouldn't make it much farther into the competition, but he was still giving everything he had. He desperately wanted to finish. By the final lap it seemed as if everyone in the stadium was on his or her feet cheering, and surely many spectators were standing in their own living rooms. His finish was an emotional moment. He'd done it. He wouldn't get a medal—but he'd still won. He won the heart of millions that day, and he won the respect of his fellow swimmers. "Press on toward the goal to win the prize for which God has called [you]" (Philippians 3:14). In all you do, do your best.

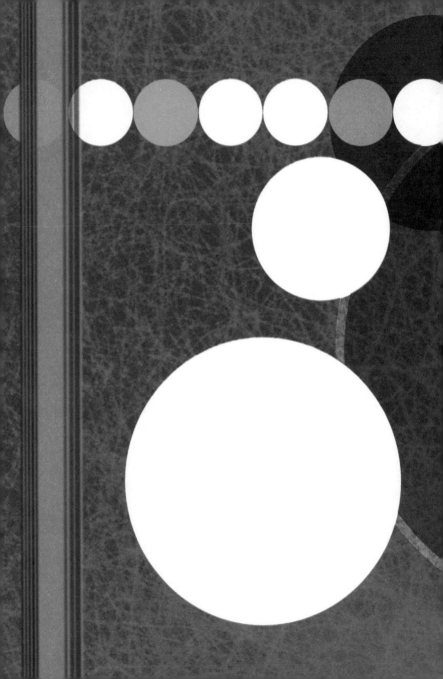

A God wise enough to create me and the world I live in is wise enough to **watch out for me.**

—Philip Yancey

Ropes Course Ranger

The alarm went off at 7:00 A.M. It felt like 5:00. The previous night had been a late one with lots of activities—s'mores, singing around the pool, and then the never-ending conversations in the bunks. But now it was morning, and with the sun streaming in through the cabin windows, there was absolutely no denying it. Mike rolled over and pulled the covers up over his head, wanting just a few more peaceful moments of rest. But Jeff and Marty, the endless-energy counselors, would have none of it.

"Everybody up!" yelled Marty, bursting with enthusiasm.

"It's ropes course day, and we've got to be out there in fifteen minutes."

"I might be a little late," Mike murmured from under the pile of blankets.

"Let's go! That means everybody," Marty retorted with a smile. "Our cabin is the first one up today. Get up, get dressed, and get moving."

Mike managed to slowly crawl out of bed and get dressed. He had heard about this ropes course; it was supposed to be pretty challenging. But when had he ever backed down from a challenge? (OK, maybe a few times.)

Soon the entire cabin of guys was headed up the trail toward the course. It was a beautiful day, and they soon saw the ropes course nestled among the trees along the hillside. From a distance, it didn't look that tough; but as they drew closer, the trees got a lot bigger and the ropes much higher.

"That's a long way down," someone from the nervous group muttered.

"Yeah, and those rocks aren't going to cushion the fall much," another replied.

The course was huge. No, it was monstrous. When the group arrived at the starting point, everyone just stood there, awe-stricken, and stared upward at the gigantic maze of ropes, ladders, cables, and bridges suspended high above them in the trees. Mike was definitely wide awake now and a little less confident than he was a few short minutes ago. The rumors were true. This thing was not going to be easy.

The boys in the cabin elected Jeff, one of their counselors, to be the first to tackle the monster. He harnessed up and led the way. Mike was a decent athlete and really wanted to get this over, so he volunteered to go next. Once harnessed in, he climbed up the first tree and headed out onto the midair course. It was pretty scary at first, but with each step he felt more at ease and his confidence increased. For the most part, Mike maneuvered the course well. He lost his footing a time or two but was able to regain his balance and press forward. The course ended with a thirty-foot free fall, controlled by someone on the ground who, by working the ropes, would bring each student to a safe and gentle landing. When he reached the end, Mike couldn't help but hesitate. It was a long way down. *One more step and I've done it,* he told himself; and with that, he stepped out into the free fall. It took him a moment to catch his breath once he had reached the ground, but Mike felt a congratulatory pat on his back from Jeff for a job well done.

Each of the other guys harnessed up in turn and proceeded through the course. Some had more difficulty than others, and each had their moments of insecurity, but they all made it through the course without much trouble. Jeff was there to greet everyone as they finished, and he slapped them on the back with a hearty "Good job."

There was only one guy left to go—Allen. He had waited until the end so he wouldn't slow anyone else down. Allen had been afflicted with cerebral palsy from birth, and there wasn't much in this life that came easily for him. Everything seemed to be a challenge.

Allen had watched all of the others, one at a time, make it through the course. He wanted desperately to complete it as well, but he knew it was going to take every ounce of energy he had. He was nervous but determined. What he may have lacked in motor skills, he made up for in courage.

Right behind Allen was their other counselor, Marty. One would be hard-pressed to find a more encouraging guy. Marty was ready and willing to assist Allen every step of the way. The two made their way onto the course and began the journey. Their pace was understandably much slower than the rest of the group members; each step was an accomplishment. Inch by painstaking inch, they made their way through the trees, up one ladder and down another. Allen was giving it all he had. They moved across another bridge and then back onto the ropes. It might take him a little longer than the others, but he was not going to quit. Marty was right beside him with unwavering patience. The two forged ahead. The rest of the group was standing below cheering them on.

"You're doing great!" one guy hollered.

"Keep it up!" came a shout from another.

As the time passed, other cabin groups arrived at the course ready to take their turn. Things were running way behind schedule, but no one seemed to mind. Many of the students shouted their encouragement to Allen while others simply looked on in disbelief. Everyone was amazed. Just when it seemed the duo couldn't make it any farther, they would find a way to manage a few more steps. They simply pressed on, no matter how hard it seemed. Eventually they reached the final stage. Before them was a rope ladder set at a forty-five-degree incline that would lead them up to the free fall. Both Allen and Marty were exhausted. The journey up to this point had nearly drained them. Both wondered if they could really make it. But they had come this far—there was no way they could stop now. Marty lay facedown on the ladder and told young Allen to "climb aboard." Allen pulled himself onto his counselor's back, and Marty began the final ascent. Rung by tiring rung, they proceeded upward, Marty climbing and Allen hanging on tight.

Finally, they reached the last platform. Only the free fall was left. By now, quite a crowd had gathered, and more and more people were cheering. Everyone knew that Allen had almost accomplished the impossible and couldn't wait for the adventure to be completed. Mike remembered his own hesitation before the jump and hollered up his words of encouragement.

"You can do it!" Mike yelled, in full belief that he could.

Not a second later, Allen closed his eyes, counted to three, and jumped.

Any fear left over from the jump was immediately replaced by an ear-to-ear grin as Allen felt the safety rope tense up, ending his free fall. As he hung there safely suspended in midair, he shouted with joy as he realized the magnitude of his achievement. He had done it! He came, he saw, and he conquered the ropes course. Jeff embraced

Allen's sweat-soaked body. Marty flung his arms around those two, and Mike and the rest of the cabin were quick to join the joyous embrace. It was hard to tell who was more excited—Allen or all the rest of them.

At dinner that night, Allen's mind-boggling achievement was all anyone could talk about. When everyone had finished eating, the camp director stepped up to the microphone. He recounted the story of the ropes course adventure earlier that day. When he had finished describing the event, he invited Allen up to the front for a special presentation. People were instantly on their feet cheering. Allen made his way forward to accept his award amid a resounding standing ovation. Mike looked around his table and saw tears welling up in the eyes of Marty and Jeff and the other guys. He couldn't hold back his own. They whistled, applauded, and cheered.

They had witnessed an incredible teenager finish an amazing feat. All who were fortunate enough to be there learned lessons in patience, trust, encouragement, and perseverance that would not soon be forgotten. And they were now witnessing the rightful recognition of a friend.

Allen beamed as he was introduced with the honorary title of "Ropes Course Ranger." He had most certainly earned it. In a world in need of heroes, none of the guys needed to look any farther than their courageous cabin mate. What he accomplished and how he went about it had inspired them all.

Taking Chances

F O U R

Give Me all your
worries, shortcomings, and
fears because I tenderly and
personally care for you.
Don't settle for mere survival.
I came to take you out of your comfort zone
into My abundant life. I'll show you
the path of life. You can't begin to imagine
all of the incredible things I've prepared for
you because you love Me.

Living on the cutting edge,
Jesus

—from 1 Peter 5:7; John 10:10
Psalm 16:11; 1 Corinthians 2:9

Taking risks can be scary. You don't know if you'll achieve your goal or fall flat on your face. Most of us have had the privilege of doing both—maybe you've had more experience in the face-plant category. But whatever the outcome, these kinds of experiences help us grow. "Crash and burn's" are not as scary as the "what if's"— never knowing what could've been. The great thing about taking a risk is that you might make it! You might accomplish something you once thought impossible, and *wow!* what a feeling. And

if you don't make it the first
time, you can always try again. But
if you never try, you'll never know.
If you don't take a chance, you could
miss out on something wonderful. Life
has so much to offer, but sometimes
you've got to be willing to step out of
your comfort zone and step into the
unknown. Who knows what you'll
discover? Who knows where it
might lead? Whatever it is,
you'll experience something
new—something all your
own, and my guess is,
you'll grow.

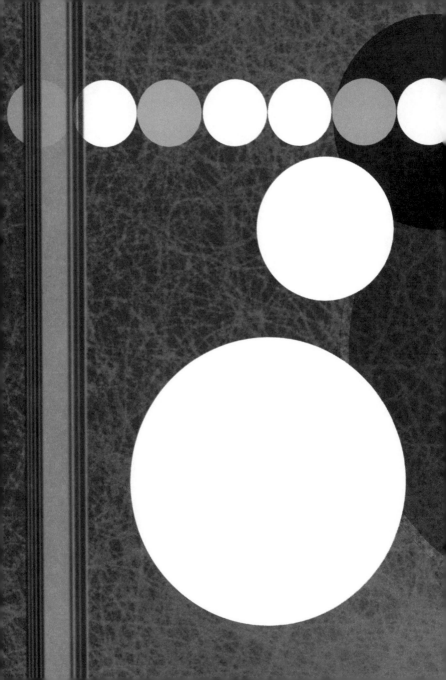

You are only one step
away from God doing a
fresh thing in your life.
**Choose to dream
His dream.**

—David Edwards

History Class

Mrs. Taylor handed back the tests one by one. She walked up and down the rows smiling at some students and offering sympathy to others. She was getting closer—the moment of truth would soon be here. Stephanie had listened in class, read the material, and studied hard. Mrs. Taylor placed the test on Stephanie's desk. Stephanie looked at the top of the page—a big red D. She got a D. She was certain the grade would be better this time—but another D—this was not happening. She was a good student, but for whatever reason, she got all flustered with history. She wanted to learn this stuff, but it was just so confusing. She felt helpless.

She had worked hard, and this was the result. What was she going to do?

She tried to cover her face; she could feel the tears coming. She wiped her eyes and somehow managed to make it through the rest of class. When the bell finally rang, Stephanie got out of that room as fast as she could.

Kayla caught up to Stephanie in the hallway. "Are you OK?" she asked. "I thought I saw you crying in there."

"Yeah, maybe a little, but I'm all right," replied Stephanie, wondering why one of the cheerleaders would be talking to her.

"History can be frustrating sometimes, huh?" Kayla said with an understanding smile.

"You can say that again."

"I know we don't know each other that well, but if you ever want someone to study with...well, history has always been fun for me, and if I can help in any way, I'd be happy to."

"I don't know. I'm trying so hard, but I'm just not getting it. I definitely need some sort of help. At this rate, I'm not sure if I'm even going to pass the class."

"I'm serious, if you want to get together, just let me know."

"OK, thanks. I'll think about it."

With that the girls went their separate ways. Stephanie went to her locker and grabbed the rest of her things. On her way home, she thought more about Kayla's offer. Why did Kayla care so much? She seemed really nice and sounded sincere, but they barely knew each other, and they ran with completely different crowds. Kayla didn't seem to mind, and Stephanie knew she needed the help. She wasn't able to do it on her own, and she needed a decent grade in that class.

The next day in class, Stephanie leaned over to Kayla, "So this stuff comes easily to you?"

"I wouldn't say it's easy. I just think it's interesting," replied Kayla.

Stephanie continued, "Can I still take you up on that offer for help?"

"Absolutely."

The girls agreed to meet at the coffee shop down the street the next day after school. When Stephanie walked in the door, she smelled a mixture of different coffee aromas and heard the sounds of workers grinding espresso behind the bar. This place was definitely hopping. Stephanie walked to the counter, ordered a vanilla latte, and proceeded to a corner table to wait for Kayla. Not more than a minute later, Kayla entered the shop. She said hi, placed her bag on the table, and went to the bar and ordered hot tea. When they were both settled, the girls chatted and got to know each other a little better. They lived only a few blocks apart but had never really spent any time together. They seemed to have quite a lot in common. The time flew by, and they finally looked at their watches and realized they had better get to work. They had come there to study.

They opened their books, and Kayla proceeded to

explain the importance of the eighteenth century. The way she talked about this stuff, anyone would find it interesting. She really got excited about the events of the past.

"We can learn so much from what went on back then—the way people related, what they cared about, and what they felt was worth fighting for. It's where we come from, and I think it can help us to see better where to go," Kayla explained.

Stephanie had never remotely thought of it that way. History was just a bunch of people, places, and dates long ago that she was supposed to memorize. But Kayla talked about these people as if they were real; she wondered what life was like for them. She had a way of bringing events of the past to life.

"I think I'm beginning to get it," Stephanie said. "You care so much about this stuff; it makes me want to care too."

"I've always found that it's easier to remember the places and dates if I try to imagine what it was like to live back then—no TV, no phones, no cars. It was so different from today—we have so much. I ask myself how we got from there to here. Thinking of history that way keeps me interested. It's like I'm an explorer, and who knows what kind of treasure I'll find?"

"Well, it's definitely working for you, so I'd be a fool not to give your approach a try," Stephanie grinned.

The girls met twice a week and read about, discussed, and studied the events of history. There was as much laughter as there was dialogue. As Stephanie and Kayla's friendship continued to grow, they found more things to talk about and more ways to help each other. Stephanie was gifted at math and offered her knowledge and insight to Kayla in that area. They enjoyed their time together and were continually amazed at how they complemented each other. They had different friends, different gifts, and different approaches, but they were able to work together and help each other in their respective areas of need.

Stephanie grew fonder of and got better at history. She

enjoyed studying the events of the past more than ever, and her grades in the subject were markedly improving. Kayla's math skills and problem solving were also getting better, and her test scores reflected this growing knowledge.

The time together was a major part of both of the girls' lives. Stephanie would come in and order her latte; Kayla, her tea; and the two would chat about boys, school, and everything else under the sun. Both of their friendship circles widened as each would at times bring others to their study table. Even with growing commitments and tight schedules, the girls made their time together a priority. And in the midst of so much to talk about, they always seemed to find time for their studies—for that was what the relationship was born from. One friend helping another; two people sharing their individual gifts for the benefit of both.

Who would have ever thought that they would become so close? What had started as one student's recognition of a classmate's need had become an incredibly strong friendship.

They had both grown so much during the year—both in their studies and as individuals. Stephanie was grateful that Kayla had taken a chance and extended the offer of help earlier in the year. If it weren't for her courage to reach out, they might never have become friends, and Stephanie might never have made it through that history class.

Supporting Friends

F I V E

**Love one another,
for love originates in Me.**
My love for you reaches
to the heavens. I've redeemed you,
intimately calling you by name. When you
go through tough times, I'm with you every
painful step. I won't let you be overwhelmed.
I'm committed to you—no matter what!
I daily bear your heartache and
hold the things that worry you.

Comforting hugs,
Your God and Friend

—from 1 John 4:7–8; Psalm 36:5
Isaiah 43:1–4; Psalm 68:19

Friends will tell you the truth, even when it hurts. They will hold your hand and stay close when you're afraid. Friends always seem to have a shoulder available for tears—and some tissue handy. They listen well and give timely hugs. Friends will walk you through the storms of life and help you look for the rainbows. With a friend, even the everyday things become memories. Whether you've known your friend for years or are just beginning the relationship, he or she seems to understand. It doesn't matter if your circle of friends is large or small—each friend is a gift from God. A friend loves you as you are and wants to get to know you better. And chances are you want to get to know your friends better too. We all have the opportunity to be a friend to many, and we'll make many new friends over the course of a lifetime. But if you could have only one friend, what an amazing friend we have in Jesus.

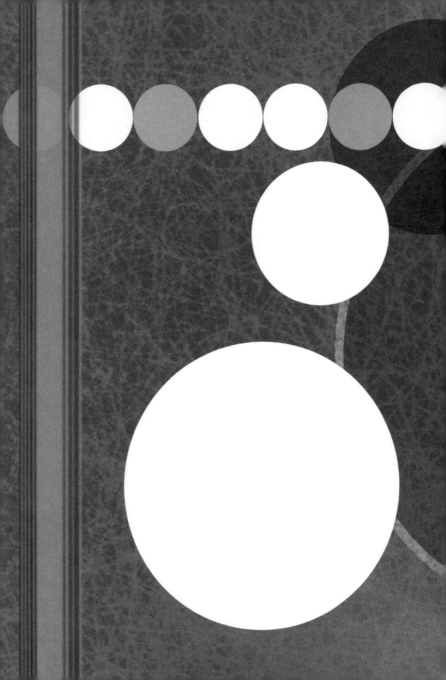

A true friend doesn't care what I've done or where I've been; there's an **unconditional commitment** that will never die.

—Michael W. Smith

Prom Date

Amber sat alone in her room crying. This was supposed to be one of the best nights of her life, and here she was with her head in her hands weeping. It was prom night, and she wasn't going. She and David had broken up just one short week ago. She knew it was the right thing to do, but this was so hard. This was her senior prom, her final high school dance, and now she didn't have a date.

David was a nice guy, and she really cared for him, but the physical part of their relationship had gone way too far. It all started innocently enough—a couple of dates and some good-night kisses. They grew to like each other and started seeing each other more frequently. Over the months, as they continued to spend time together, the kisses got longer and longer, and one thing, as it usually does, led to another. And eventually, they had gone too far.

It was consensual, but while David felt it had been the next logical step in their relationship, Amber knew it was wrong. She felt terrible. She had always planned on saving herself for the man she would marry. She had been to True Love Waits rallies and made commitments. She felt like such a hypocrite. All her friends in her youth group knew she wanted to wait, and she had made the one mistake that she didn't want to make. She wrestled with the toughest of questions: Did God still love her after what she had done? Could she love herself? What would her friends think? What would they say?

Kim and Sammie had been incredible. They had been so supportive throughout the whole ordeal. They were Amber's truest friends. They listened, they cried, and they prayed with her. They assured her that God did still love her—and that He forgave her. Jesus had died for her sins, for this sin. These were things that Amber knew and believed, but they resonated deeply during this painful time. Kim and Sammie also offered their advice. They strongly encouraged Amber to break off the relationship. It seemed to be the only option. She and David desired different things and approached life from completely different perspectives. She could see that now. But it wasn't going to be easy. Amber cared for him deeply. They had so much in common and had grown incredibly close over this past year. But she knew what she had to do, and with the loving support of her two friends, she cut the ties on a yearlong relationship.

Now it was prom night, and she was alone. Kim and Sammie encouraged her to come to the dance with them, but Amber didn't want to be a fifth wheel. She told them thanks but that she'd probably just rent a couple of movies and stay at home. Amber stared at her prom dress hanging in the corner and then looked down at the rented movies beside her bed.

The dance would be getting started about now. Just then the doorbell rang. It was Kim and Sammie. What were they doing here? Shouldn't they be at the prom? They looked amazing—their dresses were gorgeous, and they were running up the stairs smiling. They were on their way to the dance from a fancy dinner when they had the limo driver drop them off at Amber's house with orders to be back in thirty minutes. They would meet their dates at the dance later.

"We're here to kidnap you," Sammie said grinning.

"Let's get you ready to go!" said Kim as she grabbed the dress from the closet.

Amber could hardly believe it; this was too good to be true. Was she dreaming? Or could her best friends in the world really be here! The girls proceeded to make Amber look like a princess. They giggled as they did Amber's makeup. And they ohhed and ahhed as Amber put on her dress.

"We're your dates tonight!" laughed Kim.

Prom Date

"What about the guys?" asked Amber.

"They thought it was a super idea. They liked the ratio—three girls to two guys," replied Sammie.

The girls discussed which perfume to wear and picked out the perfect lipstick. And at last they were ready to go. Amber was a sight to behold. She looked absolutely stunning. She had her hair up and away from her face, and her infectious smile lit up the whole room. The lavender dress she wore complimented her crisp blue eyes and looked even more beautiful than it had in the store. Kim and Sammie had even brought her a corsage. The evening was turning our better than she could have ever imagined. The girls all headed downstairs, and Amber kissed her parents—who were holding back their tears—good-bye. The threesome ran outside, climbed into the limousine, and headed off to the dance.

When they arrived, the place was hopping. The music was loud, and there were balloons and confetti everywhere. The girls got their picture taken together, and then the two guys joined them. Amber savored each song. She listened to the words, sang along, and felt the music deep within her soul. She wanted memories of every single moment. She took mental snapshots of everything—the people, the food, and the decorations. She couldn't believe she was really here! She was having the time of her life with her friends at her senior prom.

So much had changed in just a matter of hours. She thought back to earlier in the evening when she was so sad, so lonely. Then she thought of the friends who wouldn't dream of leaving her alone on a night like this. They had not only walked with her through one of the toughest times in her life, but had taken it upon themselves to make sure she enjoyed this much-anticipated prom. Funny how the one dance she thought she'd miss turned out to be one of the best nights of her life.

As the evening was drawing to an end, Amber pulled Kim and Sammie close and hugged them tight. "You guys are the best!" Amber fought through her tears. "Thanks for making this such a wonderful night. I will treasure it forever."

They all hugged again. "You're worth it," said Sammie.

"That's what friends are for. You would've done the same for either of us in a heartbeat," echoed Kim.

The three girls walked out of the hall arm in arm. Amber was grateful for friends like Kim and Sammie—friends who were willing to go the extra mile. Friends who loved her enough to listen well and tell her the truth. Friends who knew how hard this night could have been. And friends that cared enough to kidnap her.

Shaping Memories

S I X

Experience My daily
blessings. As you give, I'll
generously give back to you.
Because of My great love and unfailing
compassion, you aren't destroyed.
**My compassions for you
are new every morning!**
I've put eternity in your heart. My faithfulness
continues through all generations.

Faithfully,
Your Lord

—from Luke 6:38; Lamentations 3:22–23
Ecclesiastes 3:11; Psalm 100:5

Life is full of surprises—not all of them good. The unexpected can be scary: There is the trauma of a pop quiz, the sinking feeling of a phone call bringing bad news, or the ache of a broken heart when a treasured relationship suddenly ends. But there are good surprises too. Everyone enjoys a good joke, a letter from an old friend that makes you smile, or a good grade on the test you thought you'd bombed. We don't know what tomorrow will bring or what surprises are in store—that's why we call them surprises. And while you don't have control over the unexpected in your own life, you do have the power to surprise someone else. You have the ability to make someone's day special and memorable. Be the bearer of a pleasant surprise. Make someone laugh or help somebody smile. A simple note or quick phone call could be just what they need. Give the gift of a surprise to someone you know today. Who knows when someone might give one back to you?

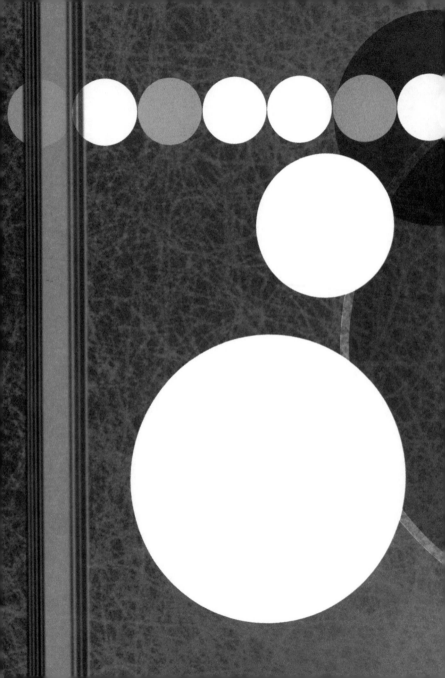

God is in the business
of taking old pieces of our
lives, refinishing them
and, at just the right time,
**surprising us with
newfound beauty.**

—Susan Duke

Birthday Present

I have loved music since I was a child. My parents noticed my interest early on and enrolled me in piano lessons. I studied classical piano for a few years and enjoyed it up to a point. My real love, though, was song writing. My brother was a songwriter, and the whole process fascinated me. The thought of pulling words and music out of thin air and trying to create something profound and beautiful was extremely intriguing. I didn't know if there was a right and a wrong way to do it or if there were rules I was supposed to follow, so I simply wrote. I wrote from my heart. I wrote from experience. I wrote about what I observed in the world around me. I heard melodies in my head and felt that it was my job to bring them to life. My first songs probably weren't much to speak of, but I liked them, and that was what mattered.

I would continually ask my brother questions and beg him to listen to my songs. I wanted to become a better writer. I would play the songs on the piano, sing my heart out, and record it all on a little boom box. The sound quality was horrible, but it was the best I could do. My brother must have realized that this was more than a hobby for me. He saw that I was engrossed in and passionate about songwriting, and he wanted to encourage me to keep going. I had always dreamed of what it would be like in a big recording studio, but I just wrote it off as something that would never happen.

Much to my amazement, on my sixteenth birthday, my big brother did the unimaginable—he rented some studio time and surprised me with the gift of a lifetime. It seemed too good to be true. Would I really get to record one of my own songs? Play the instruments? Hear my voice on tape? It was going to happen. We were going to a big-time studio to record. Unbelievable!

The next two weeks were spent working out the many details. My brother and I listened together to countless songs and finally settled on one to record. We spent time discussing the musical arrangement of the song: what the tempo would be, when the bass would come in, what keyboard sounds we should use. We planned as much as we could prior to the recording session, hoping to maximize our time in the actual studio.

Finally, the big day arrived. I was so excited. I loaded some music equipment and my keyboard into the car and headed off to the studio. My mind was racing with thoughts of what it might be like. I'd never been inside a professional studio before, so I didn't have a clue what to expect.

My brother was outside the studio, waiting for me when I drove up.

"You ready?" he asked.

"Absolutely!" I responded with unrestrained enthusiasm. And with that we headed inside.

The studio manager greeted us with pleasantries and a smile. "Tony will be your engineer today," said the manager as he led us to the control room. "He knows this room well and can help you with whatever you need."

I soon realized that Tony was the man who knew how the studio worked. He knew the purpose for every button, dial, and lever in that intimidating room. The soundboard seemed to stretch on for a mile, and I'd never seen so many expensive speakers.

"I think you'll like the sound of this place," Tony said. "It really allows you to hear the true essence of the recording."

Like it? I thought, remembering the tiny boom box I was accustomed to. *This is incredible! Any song would sound great in here!* It was a beautiful facility, complete with state-of-the-art equipment and a friendly staff.

"Well, shall we begin?" asked my brother. He, too, seemed excited.

Birthday Present

"Let's," answered Tony.

I proceeded to unload my gear and get it all hooked up. Soon we had keyboard sounds coming through the speakers, and we were ready to go.

We didn't have the time or money to have a band come in and learn the song, so my brother and I relied on programming some of the parts. First, we laid down a basic program that mapped out the song. Once that was on tape, we began to add the drums. We spent some time selecting the drum sounds we would use and eventually put them to tape. I had no idea how much time we would spend on details, but my brother and Tony assured me that the hard work would pay off in the end. Next up was the bass, followed by some keyboard parts. We listened to what we had on tape, and it sounded amazing! The sound was so crisp and big. Collectively, we decided that some guitar would be nice, so my brother strapped one on and added his part. I sat back and listened, once again marveling at how incredible the song was sounding. It was almost too good to be true—as if

I were living inside of a dream. Someone would surely wake me up sooner or later.

When the music tracks were complete, it was time to add the vocals. Tony showed me into the vocal booth and dimmed the lights.

"A lot of people like to record this way," he said.

"Works for me," I managed to respond.

Tony handed me a pair of headphones and told me how far from the microphone I should stand to get the best sound. I placed the headphones over my ears and tried to get comfortable—a feat nearly impossible considering how nervous I was. I sang a few notes into the mike and heard it instantly through the phones. The sound was incredibly clear; I could hear every little nuance of my voice. *This is scary,* I thought to myself. But soon, as Tony began to add the music tracks into the phones, everything started to fill out.

"How's the balance?" came Tony's voice through the headphones.

Birthday Present

"Sounds pretty good," I replied.

"Let's go from the top. I'll put you in record, but understand that we don't have to keep any of this. Just try to get used to the sound and give it your best," Tony's voice echoed with encouragement.

The music filled the phones, and I sang the song all the way through. I was used to sitting at the piano and belting a song out, so hearing my voice and all the music through the headphones took a little getting used to. I sang the tune through a couple more times, each time feeling more and more comfortable.

"Sounding good," said my brother from the control room. "How's it feel to you?"

"It's getting easier. Can we take it one more time?" I asked.

And with that the music began to roll. I sang my heart out. It was by far the best I'd done. Tony and my brother agreed.

"Why don't you come in here and take a listen," said Tony.

"On my way," I said, removing the headphones.

Back in the control room, we listened to the vocal. Everyone seemed to like it. Tony maneuvered a few knobs and levers and added some vocal effects. It was really sounding like a song. This was so much fun! Tony and my brother played with the mix, boosting the bass here and ducking the guitar there. And with a little more tinkering, it was complete. My first song recorded at a real studio. We listened again. It was better than I could have ever imagined.

When we were finished packing up, Tony handed me the master tapes and a personal copy of the song. "Good sounding stuff. I enjoyed it," he said.

"Thank you. Thanks for a great day."

My brother and I said our good-byes to Tony and the studio manager then headed to our cars. There in the parking lot I tried to thank my brother for an unbelievable day. He would probably never understand what this day had meant to me—what a dream come true it was. I told him how much I enjoyed the whole process and how amazing the day had been. He just smiled a knowing smile.

My brother believed in my dreams enough to take action, and he opened up a door to a new world of possibilities. He saw my love for something and helped it grow. And he enabled me to live out a dream. It was an incredible birthday present from an incredible brother, and I am grateful.

Making a Difference

SEVEN

103

In light of My
awesome promises, turn away
from everything wrong and live
purely with My help.
Focus on truth—
whatever is noble, whatever is right,
whatever is lovely, whatever is admirable—and
anything that is excellent or praiseworthy!
I am able to keep you on track and to stop you
from falling during enticing temptation.
I'll make you stand firmly,
without fault and in My presence.

Gloriously,
Your God of Victory

—from 2 Corinthians 7:1
Philippians 4:8
Jude 24

What do you believe in? What are you passionate about? What sort of things do you stand for? The things we believe in and the things we are passionate about help to shape who we are and the decisions we make. They affect our choices and define our dreams. The things you believe in and stand for may not always be popular. People may laugh at you, tell you you're crazy, or call you a fool. But you wouldn't be alone. Many people thought Jesus was crazy because of the things He said and believed. There were many who mocked Him and some who believed He was dangerous. But in spite of the opposition and the disbelief, He stayed the course and persevered. Jesus believed in His Father's plan enough to sacrifice His life, suffer, and die on a cross. And He did it because He was passionate about you and me.

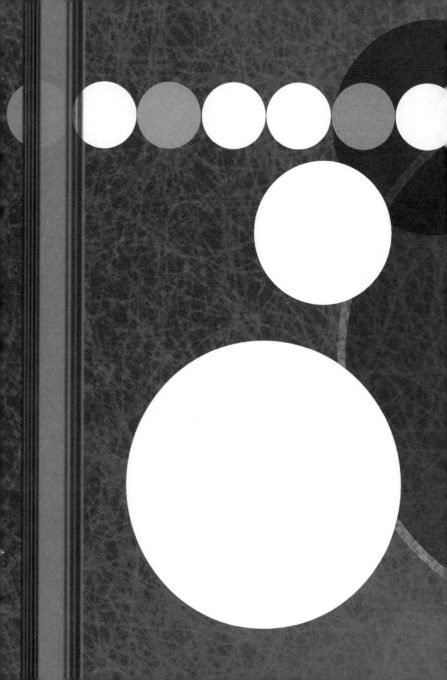

When we get our
minds focused on the
basics of life,
we see that in reality
wrong is still wrong and
right is still right and
God is still in control.

—Kirk Sullivan, 4HIM

The Goal

Graduation was just around the corner, with only a few days of school remaining. The girls had been meeting for almost a year now. Every Monday morning at six, Julie, Erin, Shelby, and Kirsten would get together at Melissa's house for breakfast, a Bible study, and to simply share what was going on in their lives. They were all in the same cabin at camp last summer. Melissa was one of the counselors, and the four girls had each made recent decisions to follow Christ, accepting Jesus as their Lord and Savior.

Melissa knew that these baby Christians had much to learn, and she wanted to share the bits of knowledge and wisdom she had gained through her years of following Jesus. Julie, Erin, Shelby, and Kirsten were all seniors, and Melissa knew that this year would be full of choices. She understood how crucial it was to lay a strong foundation in Christ. She knew the importance of studying God's Word, asking questions, and having a mentor. Someone had mentored her, and she wanted to do the same for these young women.

During their first time together, Melissa asked each of the girls to set some goals for the year, both as a group and personally. After some time of thought, Julie decided that her goal for the group was for them to dive deep into the Word of God—to learn as much as they could in their first year as Christians. Her personal goal was to make it through her senior year without drinking any alcohol. The party scene around school was booming, and she had been a frequent guest at the events in the past. She would no doubt be invited to some huge parties, and she would most certainly be tempted; but she wanted to try.

The Goal

Not only was she underage—making drinking with her friends illegal—she just knew it was something she shouldn't do. God was changing her life, and she wanted to take a stand. So this would be her goal. She knew she would need the support and encouragement of the other girls to make it, so she shared her goal with the group. All of the girls were incredibly supportive. One by one, each of the others made it one of their goals as well. They would do it together.

Now, with one week of school left, this was their final Monday together. Each of them had encountered some rough moments during the year. Mistakes had been made, confessions shared, and forgiveness granted. But, so far, all of the girls had been successful in their goal not to consume alcohol. Many graduation bashes were scheduled for the coming week, and the girls knew that the peer pressure and temptation to drink would be incredibly high. They prayed for strength. They had made it this far; they wanted to finish strong.

Finally, graduation night was upon them—the culmination of so many years of school. They had made it. So many classes, so many tests, so many friends, and so many memories. It was overwhelming. This chapter of their lives was quickly coming to a close. The ceremony included a few speeches and the customary moving of the tassel. Hats were thrown into the air, and the celebrations began. Many all-night gatherings and numerous parties were scheduled. The four girls wanted to spend this special night with their friends, and the gathering of choice was a big bonfire at the beach.

By the time the girls arrived, the party was in full swing. The fire was hot, the music was loud, and the alcohol was readily available. There were hundreds of students there, and most of them seemed to be drinking. This was not going to be easy, but they hadn't expected it to be. They had prepared for a battle, for a tough night, and they were determined to make it through.

Almost as soon as they got to the bonfire site, someone

offered Julie a beer; she responded politely with a "No thanks." There was a part of her that wanted to have just one drink—one toast to finally making it through twelve years of school. But she was very aware of the commitment she had made to herself, her friends, and to God. Julie knew she was being prayed for just as she was praying for her friends on this night. She also knew that others, some she knew of and some people she didn't, were watching the decisions and choices she made. She recalled the verse she had learned in Philippians—"I can do all things through Christ who gives me strength"—and she drew upon the strength of her Lord in every way that she knew.

There were other times of temptation throughout the night, but each girl was always ready to help the other. A quick word, an encouraging scripture, a gentle reminder—they did whatever it took to make it through the night. Julie was hanging with Kirsten, and Erin was chatting with Shelby and a couple of guys, then later different pairs would form. But not one of them was on their own at any time during the evening. At one point, Julie's cell phone rang. It was Melissa offering her support. She was calling to congratulate them and to let them know that she was praying for them even as they spoke. The girls were there for each other and because of that unity were able to take a stand. Some of the other students asked them why they weren't drinking—especially on a night like this—and they had several opportunities to share their faith and talk about what they believed and why they were making these choices. Who knows what seeds were planted, what lives may have been touched? All in all, Kirsten, Shelby, Erin, and Julie enjoyed a wonderful evening of celebration, and not one of them had a single drink.

As the sun was coming up, Julie said a prayer of thanks—thanks to God for taking care of each of them on such a pivotal night, for walking with them and holding them close when they needed it most. By His grace and with the support of a now very well-knit group, she had taken a stand for Christ this senior year. And in some small way, she believed she had made a difference, but she certainly couldn't have done it by herself. All four girls had set the same goal, and all had achieved it.

They had supported and encouraged one another. When one was weak, the others were strong. They listened and they learned from their mentor, Melissa. They pointed each other toward God and His desire for their lives. They took a stand for Christ, and they chose the foundation of their faith over the pressure of their peers.

Remember your Creator

in the days of your youth.

—Ecclesiastes 12:1